You Are Magical Vol.1

J.J. Ems

This book is dedicated to the seekers who walk the path less traveled. Within these pages, you will find the keys to mental clarity, the gateway to endless possibilities, and the foundation of true freedom.

Know that you are seen, you are enough, and you are loved.

Contents

WELCOME
TO THE
MAGIC

Welcome!

You were always meant to be here!

Hey there, magical soul.

I'm J.J. Ems, and chances are, if you've come across this guidebook to daily magical living, you most likely identify with the outcasts, the misfits, the ones who just don't quite fit in.

I know I sure do, and that's exactly why I created this guide. For all of us who think a little differently, but still want to live our lives as happily and peacefully as we can.

This book was created for anyone who has ever felt invisible, different, or tired of carrying the weight alone.

A Little About Me

I'm a freelance writer from New England. I discovered creative writing when I decided to head back to university and was encouraged by a professor to explore it further.

Before that, I always wrote, mostly in the notes on my phone, scribbling poetry, thoughts, and emotions. I'm sure a few of you reading this can relate.

Further down the line, I took a creative writing course and self-published my first novel, mostly for fun and to prove to myself that I could accomplish something I had always dreamed about.

After that, I explored different platforms, writing articles, newsletters, short stories, and various creative projects.

Throughout all of it, one thing remained the same. I always wanted to include an element of magic.

In my life experiences so far, I've explored many different spiritual practices, never limiting myself to one organized belief system, but instead embracing what truly works for me.

Alongside the mystical elements, I've always wanted to use my stories and my voice to reach people who may feel out of place or different. Those who still want to find comfort, healing, and spirituality in their own unique way.

So, my dear reader, here we are.

I've decided to put together a creative collection of short works designed to help you find light in darker days.

As someone who openly struggles with anxiety and depression in daily life, I know how hard it can be to find motivation, to get up and keep going, or to make peace with moments that feel overwhelming.

Because of my love for finding magic in everyday life, I hope these themed works can bring a little enchantment, comfort, and calm into your own daily journey.

What You Can Expect to Find Here:

❖ PART ONE – POTIONS FOR THE SOUL

A small collection of simple rituals for self-love.

❖ PART TWO – SPELLS OF MINDFULNESS (These are not actual magickal spells)

Gentle exercises to help you remain mindful and grounded.

❖ PART THREE – STORIES OF MAGIC & HEALING

Short stories with magical themes focused on emotional growth and comfort.

❖ PART FOUR - RECIPES FOR A MAGICAL LIFE

Helpful tips and daily practices written in the form of creative recipes.

❖ PART FIVE – FOR THE OUTCASTS

Short letters written just for you, for those hard days when you need a reminder to stand out proudly and wave that freedom flag.

❖ PART SIX – STAY MAGICAL

A short goodbye.

Before you dive in, I want to take a moment to truly thank you for being here with me.

Thank you for taking this journey and being willing to do the work of self-reflection and healing.

You are not alone.

We are all universally connected.

- **J.J. Ems**

Potions

✧ ✧ ✧

☾ Potions for the Soul ☽

✧ ✧ ✧

Welcome, my magical friend.

Here you will find simple rituals, decorated as potions, with tips, quotes, and gentle guidance to help you through the rougher days.

Always remember, even when things feel tough, you have the power within you to create change, no matter how small it may seem.

I wish you luck on your healing journey.

Take a sip, explore your mind, and let the magic happen.

With love and light,

- **J.J. Ems**

Potion for Self-love

"Freewill is the greatest gift when paired with human life. We get to make choices and explore the world in hopes of fulfilling our hearts' desires. Along this journey, remember to use the power of choice to love yourself."

Whatever you might be facing, a healthier, happier you will make your battle fiercer. It's never selfish to take time to reflect and appreciate your tenacity. Reflect on what you've accomplished so far, even when you thought you never could.

Love yourself for it.

✧ ✧ ✧
☾ Potion for Self-Love ☽
✧ ✧ ✧

Purpose: To appreciate the bad-ass reflection staring back at you.

Ingredients:
• A warm drink of your choice (teas work wonderfully, especially lavender for calming and rose for love)
• One quiet atmosphere
• Controlled breathing
• Comfort items (symbolic items like jewelry, plushies, or books work well)
• An uneasy thought you can gently release
• A mirror

Instructions:

Hold your warm drink in your hands.

Exhale and relax, letting the warmth comfort you as you envision your inner light awakening.

Think of the thought you are trying to release and begin a controlled breathing method of your choice. (I recommend the 4-7-8 method: inhale for four, hold for seven, exhale for eight.)

Look into the mirror and appreciate the beautiful human being you are.

When you are ready, picture that uneasy thought leaving and replace it with a challenge you have already overcome.

Embrace the relief you felt when you rose above it. Sit in that moment and remind your reflection that you are capable of doing it again.

Continue breathing and remain here as long as you need.

When you're finished, treat yourself.

Take a snack, a piece of chocolate, an apple, whatever your vibe. Remember, you're in control here.

Side effects may include:

✦ A feeling of calm

✦ A sense of self-empowerment

✦ An inner knowing that you will make it through

Potion for Peace

"A quiet mind is the key to unlocking inner peace."

Everyday tasks can be draining. When creating your task list, remember to pencil in time for yourself.

✧ ✧ ✧

☾ Potion for Peace ☽

✧ ✧ ✧

Purpose: To remain present and cultivate a sense of inner calm.

Ingredients:

• Water or a drink of your choice (Tip: If using water, a common practice is to hold the container in your hands and envision your intention flowing into it before drinking. You may imagine a peaceful state of mind and an iridescent light entering the water.)

• A quiet space

• An item that represents calm to you (a plush, a photo, a pillow, or anything comforting)

• Controlled breathing

• A mental image of a peaceful place (a lake, a snowy cabin, a quiet park)

Instructions:

Get comfortable in your quiet space and begin controlled breathing.

Once your breath feels steady, you may choose to place intention into your water. Envision a soft, iridescent light flowing from above and gently entering the top of your head.

Visualize that calming energy moving through your body and into the water through your hands.

Remain here as long as you need until it feels complete.

Take a sip of the water and imagine that same light filling you from within, spreading peace throughout your body. You may continue sipping or save the water until the end. This is your magic. Do it your way.

When ready, close your eyes and bring your chosen place of peace into your mind.

Engage with the space fully.

Consider these points:

• How does it smell?

• How does the air feel?

• Is there grass or snow?

• Is it light or dark?

Spend as much time here as you like. This place can become not only a space of peace but a place of power that you may return to whenever you need.

When you feel complete, stand up and gently shake out your body to release and ground yourself.

Side effects may include:

✦ A sense of creativity

✦ A feeling of tranquility

✦ A gentle boost in mood

Potion for Courage

"Courage is picking up the broken pieces and creating something new."

Life is not always easy. Challenges will appear when you least expect them. Growth happens when you keep moving forward despite difficult conditions and face the roadblocks in your path.

✧ ✧ ✧

☾ Potion for Courage ☽

✧ ✧ ✧

Purpose: To remember that you already hold the inner power to rise above your challenges.

Ingredients:

• Water or tea (If using tea, you can explore courage-focused blends for extra herbal support.)

• Incense of your choice (I personally prefer Dragon's Blood.)

• A quiet space

• A character you find empowering — someone who represents courage to you (from a book, movie, or anywhere else)

• Controlled breathing

Instructions:

Light your incense if using.

Settle into your quiet space and take a sip of your water or tea.

If using tea, embrace the warmth and let it comfort you. If using water, focus on its freshness and imagine a feeling of renewal entering your body.

Begin your controlled breathing until your body feels calm.

When ready, close your eyes and envision your chosen character — especially the moment where they showed courage.

Step into that scene. Imagine yourself as them. Feel the strength, the resilience, the triumph of moving through the challenge.

Sit with this feeling for as long as you need.

When you are ready, stand and do a small shake to ground yourself, reminding your body that you also carry that courage within you.

<u>Side effects may include:</u>

◆ A sense of relief

◆ A feeling of empowerment

◆ A renewed sense of courage

Potion for Letting Go

"It wasn't until I released what I have been carrying that I finally felt weightless and free."

Letting go can be difficult. As we move through life, we encounter experiences that feel heavy, and the longer we hold them, the more they tend to hurt.

I know it can be hard, but remember: the moment you choose to release those experiences is the moment healing truly begins.

✧ ✧ ✧
☾ **Potion for Letting Go** ☽
✧ ✧ ✧

Purpose: To release experiences that may be weighing on you and reconnect with your inner strength.

Ingredients:
- A warm tea for comfort (Chamomile is a calming choice.)
- A quiet space at a desk or table
- A notebook and writing utensil
- A favorite photo of yourself
- Controlled breathing

Instructions:

Take a seat at your desk or table.

Sip your tea and allow yourself to settle into the space.

Place your favorite photo where you can clearly see it.

Begin your controlled breathing until you feel calm and grounded. (The 4-7-8 method works well for this.)

Open your notebook and think about the experience you are ready to release.

Write freely about how it made you feel. Take your time and let the emotion flow onto the page.

When you are finished, look at your photo. Remember how that moment felt and why you chose it.

Remind yourself that you are beautiful and imagine an iridescent light flowing from the photo toward you. Sit with this feeling for as long as you need. It is okay if it becomes emotional. This is a moment of release.

When ready, return to your writing. Picture that same light moving through you, into your hand, and into your pen. Slowly cross out what you have written.

You are not those things. You are not those emotions.

Discard the paper if you wish. Take one last look at your photo and feel your personal power. You choose what defines you.

When you are ready, stand and shake your body gently to ground yourself.

<u>Side effects may include:</u>

✦ A feeling of rebellion

✦ A renewed sense of personal power

✦ A feeling of love and light

Potion for Healing

"Healing is finally deciding to bloom and blossom in the same soil that once attempted to bury you."

Painful experiences are meant to teach us lifelong lessons. I know it hurts, but you have the power to rise through it and continue shining your light.

✧ ✧ ✧
☾ Potion for Healing ☽
✧ ✧ ✧

Purpose: To awaken and illuminate your inner light.

Ingredients:
- Headphones
- A healing frequency instrumental that resonates with you
- An item that brings comfort
- Controlled breathing

Instructions:
Take a seat or lie down — whichever feels most comfortable. Turn on your chosen frequency. Begin your controlled breathing method of choice.

Hold your comfort item and embody the safe, joyous feeling it brings you. Let that feeling settle into your chest.

Close your eyes and think of a positive memory — a moment that made you genuinely smile. Recreate that feeling. Sit with it. Let the music sink in.

If you'd like, picture a warm light rising slowly from your feet, traveling upward through your body. Feel it drawing healing energy from the earth as it moves, washing away heaviness and restoring clarity.

Stay in this moment as long as you need.

When you're ready, gently stand and shake your body to ground yourself. If you're doing this at night, allow yourself to drift into rest and wake up refreshed.

<u>Side effects may include:</u>

◆ A lighter state of mind

◆ A feeling of relaxation

◆ An aura of Bad-Ass Energy

Potion for Confidence

"True confidence is being comfortable in your own skin and knowing you belong, whether the rest of the world likes it or not."

I can tell you from experience, my rebellious trendsetter, people get the most uncomfortable when you refuse to fit in and your light still shines. Never dim it. If anything... let them go blind.

✧ ✧ ✧

☾ **Potion for Confidence** ☽

✧ ✧ ✧

Purpose: To thrive and shine in your own skin.

Ingredients:
- A body wash or soap that comforts you
- Headphones or a speaker
- A frequency instrumental, or playlist that uplifts you
- A warm shower
- Incense of choice or a smudging tool (optional, with airflow)

Instructions:

Turn on the water and let it reach a temperature that feels just right for you.

Start your music and light your incense or smudge stick, if using.

Step into the shower and let the water run over your body. Take a moment to settle into the warmth.

Close your eyes and imagine the water washing away anything heavy or negative, letting it flow down the drain.

Picture the water glowing in a color that resonates with you, soaking into your skin and filling you with confidence and clarity.

Visualize yourself becoming brighter, more confident, and more radiant. Feel your energy expand outward, steady and undeniable.

Stay in this moment as long as you need, then continue your shower as usual.

When you step out, carry this energy with you. You are powerful. You are seen. You belong here, exactly as you are.

<u>Side effects may include:</u>

✦ A sense of empowerment

✦ A feeling of relief

✦ A quiet, unshakable confidence

Potion for Rest

"The best results come from a well-rested mind. Replenish your inner resources so you can show up at your best."

When we take time to relax and recharge, our subconscious gets the chance to run freely. With a little intention, your dreams can take you on an amazing ride.

✧ ✧ ✧

☾ **Potion for Rest** ☽

✧ ✧ ✧

This is not a traditional magick spell. It is a tool to help you embrace the full experience of a good night's sleep.

Purpose: To explore your subconscious and give your mind the rest it truly deserves.

Ingredients:

• A cup of sleepy tea (mugwort is great if you're up for some lucid dreaming)

• Your comfy bed

• Headphones

• A guided sleep meditation

• A writing utensil and journal or notepad placed nearby

Instructions:

Sip your tea as you prepare to get comfortable for bed. This is also a good time to find a guided sleep meditation that feels right for you. There are plenty of free ones out there.

If you're planning to try lucid dreaming, take a moment to jot down what you'd like to dream about. It adds a layer of intention and helps bring awareness to your subconscious.

Once you're in bed, put in your headphones and begin the meditation.

Don't stress if thoughts come and go. That's normal. Just gently bring your focus back and allow yourself to drift.

When you wake up, try to journal your dreams right away while they're still fresh.

Write down what you experienced and take a moment to appreciate the new day ahead.

If lucid dreaming doesn't happen right away, don't get frustrated. It takes practice, but once it clicks, it's a whole different level.

<u>Side effects may include:</u>

✦ An increased interest in dreaming

✦ A sense that you have more control than you thought

✦ A reminder that your mind is a pretty powerful place to be

Spells

☾ Spells ☽

Welcome back.

We've arrived at the Spells section of our magical journey together.

The rituals you'll find here are not traditional magick. They are simply tools for getting through the day, for transforming heavy energy into something lighter and more intentional.

These reminders are dressed as "spells" to keep things playful and fresh.

Feel free to add your own tools from your personal how-to-survive workshop.

Make each spell uniquely yours.

Inside, you'll find small practices I return to when I need grounding, clarity, or peace.

Have fun, my little astral traveler.

Love and Light,

- **J.J. Ems**

Calming Spell

"Anyone can get swept up in a storm of chaos, but it takes a true warrior to stand strong within it and weather the storm."

Some moments trigger reactions — it's only human.

Deciding what action you take in difficult moments defines the kind of human you choose to be.

✧ ✧ ✧

☾ Calming Spell ☽

✧ ✧ ✧

This is not a spell in the traditional sense.

It is a tool to help you return to a calm and centered state of mind.

Purpose:

To transform angry or anxious energy into a calm, productive state.

You Will Need:

- A notebook or coloring sheet
- A pen, crayons, or markers
- Controlled breathing
- An open mind
- A quiet space

Affirmations (optional):

I embody the power of transformation.

I control my destiny.

I am here, and I choose to make a change.

The Spell:

(For added calm, you may choose to work by candlelight or moonlight.)

(Feel free to repeat the affirmations above or create your own.)

Begin by sitting in a quiet space and using the controlled breathing method of your choice.

Once you feel centered, open your notebook or pick up your coloring sheet.

Set an intention within your mind to remain calm, allowing anger or anxiety to release through the act of creation.

Choose what feels right for you. You may draw a symbol, write freely, or color without expectation.

As you create, imagine your uncomfortable energy flowing into your work.

Witness the transformation. You are taking something heavy and turning it into something meaningful.

This is powerful. You are magic. You are a creator.

Remain here as long as you need — creating, reflecting, or simply sitting with what you've made.

(Depending on your style, you may choose to release your creation afterward or keep it as a reminder of your strength. Over time, you may even find yourself with a collection of art born from transformation.)

When to Use This Spell:

• When emotions feel overwhelming

• Before beginning a creative project

• When anger feels like too much

Side Effects May Include:

✦ A sense of calm

✦ A spark of creativity

✦ A feeling of self-empowerment

Spell To Calm Anxiety

"Fear visits us all. When it roars, you are allowed to soften the sound."

Life is unpredictable, and with that comes worry. We all face real problems every day, but the best way to approach them is with a clear mind. It's not over yet. We're still here, still fighting.

✧ ✧ ✧

☾ Spell To Calm Anxiety ☽

✧ ✧ ✧

This is not a traditional magick spell. It is a grounding tool to help you move through overwhelming moments with clarity.

Purpose: To create calm and think through challenges without the mental noise.

You Will Need:

• A controlled breathing method of your choice

• A quiet space

• A notebook and a pen

• Sour candy (optional — helpful for grounding the senses)

Affirmations (optional): Every problem has a solution. I will make it through this. Tomorrow is a brand new day.

The Spell:

For this exercise, focus on one problem at a time. If you feel called to work through more, you may, but start small. Remember: You Are Magical.

Begin by settling into your quiet space. Sit comfortably, whether at a desk, table, or in your bed. If using sour candy, have it nearby and begin your controlled breathing until your body feels steady.

Now write down the problem causing your anxiety.

Draw a line from it and write the outcome you fear most.

From that feared outcome, draw at least three more lines. Write potential outcomes that are opposite or positive.

Look at the page.

There is power in it.

Anxiety narrows your vision, but reality holds many possibilities. Even when something feels hopeless, there are multiple paths forward.

Worry is normal. But so is resilience.

And if the worst does happen, you will still make it through. The next day may hold surprises you cannot yet see.

When to Use This Spell:
• When a problem feels overwhelming
• When your thoughts spiral toward negative outcomes
• When you need proof that several possibilities exist

Side effects may include:
✦ A new perspective
✦ A release of mental strain
✦ A slight sugar rush

Spell For Bad Days

"Rainy days are required to bring forth some of the most beautiful plants in the world. You are a beautiful creation, too, so don't be afraid to frolic in the storm. It will pass."

Bad days are unavoidable. We all have to move through them, learn from them, and grow stronger because of them.

One of the best questions I've ever been asked is this: Out of all the bad things you think about... how many of them actually happen?

It's just a day, my friend. You will prevail.

✧ ✧ ✧

☾ Spell For Bad Days ☽

✧ ✧ ✧

This is not a traditional magick spell. It is a tool to help you move through overwhelming moments and reconnect with your imagination, even if only for a little while.

Purpose: To step away for a moment and remember what it feels like to dream. (This is one of my personal favorites.)

You will need:

- A drink of your choice (warm drinks can be especially comforting)

- A quiet space

- A book of your choice

- An open mind and a willingness to play

The Spell:

Get comfortable in your space and settle in with your chosen reading material. Fiction, fantasy, mystery — whatever calls to you. (Maybe even a short story from this book... wink wink.)

Once you're settled, take a moment to breathe and allow yourself to release some of the weight of the day.

If you enjoy music, soft instrumentals or frequency-based sounds can help you ease into the moment and create a peaceful atmosphere.

When you begin reading, allow yourself to fully immerse in the story. This is your chance to step into another world for a while.

Let your mind create the scenes. Let yourself become part of the story.

If you'd like, imagine yourself as the main character. Experience the world through their eyes.

Spend as much time as you need here.

This is your reminder that even fictional characters face challenges, and they often come out stronger on the other side.

When you're ready, gently return to the present.

You can ground yourself by choosing a category and naming as many related things as you can.

When to Use This Spell:

• When you need a temporary escape

• When your thoughts feel overwhelming

• When the day just isn't going your way

Side effects may include:

✦ A feeling of courage

✦ A sense that everything will be okay

✦ A reminder that you are the creator, and you have the power to create change

Spell for Self-Trust

"It's easy to get lost in showing up for others while navigating the busier days of life, but don't forget to show up for yourself as well. You know how the saying goes: you have to put on your own mask first before helping someone else."

Make a promise to yourself and keep it. Let that trust travel between your mind, body, and soul.

✧ ✧ ✧

☾ Spell for Self-Trust ☽

✧ ✧ ✧

This is not a traditional magick spell. It is a tool to help you show up for yourself every day. Self-care matters.

Purpose: To rebuild or strengthen trust with your true self.

You Will Need:

• An open mind

• A mirror

• An affirmation of your choice

• An app to set reminders (optional)

The Spell:

Get comfortable and think of an affirmation, or a few, that generate positive thoughts within you.(Examples: I am beautiful. I am intelligent. I am abundant.)

Once your affirmations are selected, stand in front of a mirror.

Take a calming breath and really look at yourself.

Pick out your favorite features and sit with them for a moment. Yeah, I said it, actually, admire yourself. You're allowed to.

Begin saying your affirmation(s) while focusing on those qualities.

Stay here as long as you need. Let that energy build. Let yourself glow a little louder than usual.

When you're ready, take a few calming breaths and remind yourself you're coming back to this. You made a promise, keep it.

Use a grounding technique to bring yourself back to the present, and walk away remembering the pact you made with yourself.

You can track your progress with a journal or an app and add reminders if that helps.

And listen, life happens. If you miss a day or two, don't spiral. This isn't about being perfect, it's about showing up and proving to yourself that you actually have your own back.

When to Use This Spell:

• As often as possible to make time for yourself daily

• When life feels chaotic and you need to pull your power back

• When you need a reminder of who you actually are

Side Effects May Include:

✦ A spike in self-respect

✦ Awesomeness levels rising

✦ A sudden realization that you're an effing rockstar

This page exists.
Because it's supposed to.
It doesn't need to fit the structure.
It doesn't need to have a reason.
It just is.

Short Stories

Well, if it isn't my favorite rule breaker,

It looks like we've arrived at the short story segment of our magical little journey.

Yes, in this non-fiction book, we're about to dive into fiction. Because why not? Who said we had to stay in one lane?

Not us.

We're original. We're bold.

Up next, you'll meet a few more outcasts — souls who discovered that being different might just be their greatest strength.

See? I told you that you were a rockstar.

Love and Light,

- **J.J. Ems**

Midnight Shine

*I*f only I were normal, then maybe I could appreciate the appeal of living in the Caribbean as most people on the island do.

I'd be calmed by the cool breeze and comforted by the warm tropical sun.

I'd probably be fixated on the clear blue ocean, the warm sand crunching beneath my feet, or even the tropical scents arising from the jerk pits as family and friends gather in celebration alongside the bewitching beaches.

If everything were different, maybe I'd even be lucky enough to dance freely to the beats of my country, body swaying in pride and freedom, completely oblivious to anyone's differences, too busy being entirely lost in paradise.

But I'm not that fortunate; I can't focus on the cuisine, the music, or the culture; I can only focus on one thing: masking my glow.

It's happened to me for as long as I can remember, since I was a child: *the illumination.*

When things felt too heavy, when I got too excited, or just whenever the emotions became too much; I emanated a glow, causing disruption, marking me as different, causing me to feel alone.

If everything were perfect, maybe people would try to understand it, or maybe make me feel less like a spectacle and an actual part of their world.

Instead, they mocked, they jeered, they laughed, making me feel emptier and creating an inner desire to diminish my shine.

I spent years trying to diminish it until I found a sense of control, becoming numb and robotic just to function in society unnoticed; less afraid.

I try not to feel anything too deeply, or again, here comes the glow, then the crowd, then the pain.

I couldn't take it anymore. I had to find someone, anyone who could help, and that's when I found her, Dr. Michaels, my therapist, who, of course, never had a patient who had the same inner light.

Although this is only our second meeting, this time feels different. I try to remain calm as I settle into my sofa, log into the online therapy portal, and wait for her to sign in.

Her face brings life to the waiting room screen, followed by the warm tone of her voice as our session begins.

"Hello, Spencer, how are you doing today?" she asks softly.

"I'm okay," I reply dryly, only to satiate her opening question.

I notice her eyes surveying the screen deeply. I assume she's looking through previous notes. I wait patiently for her to continue the conversation.

"So, Spencer, last time we talked, you mentioned that you haven't been that social, due to the glow. I recommended you reach out to at least one person and strike up a conversation. Were you able to do that?"

"Yes," I lie, keeping my response short and simple, again hoping to just answer her question with a viable response.

"Great, tell me about it," she replies enthusiastically, and I feel my heart drop.

I try searching my brain for a response, but I feel it erupting from within me; I can't control it; it starts as a slight shimmer, and I start to grow warm, the heat rises, and I become iridescent — I begin to glow.

Her eyes grow wide. I've only told her about my condition. I'm usually in control, but I've been so overwhelmed with emotions lately that it escaped. I focus and dim it back down, slowly, and I feel the coolness replacing the heat, stabilizing my affliction, giving me back control.

"I—I'm sorry, I—can't control it sometimes it just..."

She interrupts.

"Don't be sorry, Spencer. I honestly have never seen anything like it, but I will break the rules a bit here and tell you one thing: it's beautiful."

"Now, gauging by your response, I'm assuming you haven't attempted to contact a friend as recommended. Are you at least still writing? I know you said that helped."

Writing...

It's all I have to stop the glow to keep it under control.

I push away my thoughts and muster up a response.

"Yes, I write a lot."

"And you said it helps you control the glow, right?" she asks.

"Yes, it's the only thing that works when it's too overwhelming."

"Okay, so how about this? Why not try going out, but bring a journal or notebook with you, just in case you feel like you need to maintain composure? You can do this. Think of it as a safety net, before you know it, you might not even need it anymore, or better yet, maybe it'll help you embrace your glow instead of hiding it," she states, sweetly, but still in a matter-of-fact kind of way.

"Okay," I respond in my now signature dry tone.

"Alright, Spencer, is there anything else you want to go over this session before we wrap things up?"

"No, that's it." I blurt out.

"Okay, see you next month?"

"See ya," I respond and close out the therapy session.

My thoughts are racing as I get ready for bed. She insists on my being social, but to me, that's a nightmare. I can't help but think of every possible thing that might go wrong, every situation that might cause me to glow.

As I settle into my bed, my final thoughts help me decide. I can't run forever; I will always have my light.

Maybe she's right...

I could try. If I panic, I can always leave...

There is that beach party tomorrow night, and the area's pretty open...

I should be okay there...

The next day went by quickly; all I could think about was the party and how I was going to do this, how I had to face my fear.

I picked out a simple outfit: a navy polo and black cargo pants so I could blend comfortably into the night.

I combed my messy black fade and slapped down gel to achieve a clean and sleek look, the kind that won't draw attention and can allow a person to easily sneak away unnoticed.

Once casually content with my look, I grabbed my journal and pen as Dr. Michaels suggested, and as I clutched them in my hand, I instantly felt a bit more at ease.

The cab ride was quiet, and as I exited the car and approached the beach, I felt a sense of panic begin to bubble within the depths of my stomach.

The laughter, the running people, I don't belong, I'm not like them. They don't know what it feels like to be this afraid; they don't know what it feels like to glow.

It sneaks its way in, the warmth before the shimmer, and I quickly open my notebook and write two simple words: Not today. I slam it shut with authority; I can do this.

I have to try...

I promised Dr. Michaels...

Making my way onto the beach, I notice a small wooden picnic table, lonely and abandoned. I choose to sit there; it looks like we could both use a friend.

I open my notebook and begin to write:

On a beach, he took a chance

Where the moon wasn't afraid to glow

He looked to the sky for guidance

Heart filled with envy

Due to the moon's courage

To glitter...

"Hi!" an unfamiliar voice interrupts my writing, sending a shock of panic through my soul.

"U-h, uh hi," I respond, still focused on the unfinished page, voice shaky, afraid to shimmer.

"What are you writing?" the voice asks, tone deep and soothing. I look up from the page and see a guy like me, simply dressed, poised, and soft-spoken.

"Just scribbling," I respond, getting lost in the gloss of his eyes, which seem pure and innocent, full of life and full of love.

"May I?" he asks, taking a seat next to me, his hand out-held.

I silently nod and hand him my journal, being vulnerable for the first time in a long time, sharing a piece of my world with a stranger.

It's impossible not to watch as his face responds to my writing. I stare, intrigued for moments, until he finally breaks the silence.

"There are more of us, you know," he states while flipping pages.

"Huh?" I ask genuinely curious.

"Your writing is beautiful. Follow me," he offers, closing my journal and handing it back to me.

"Uh, okay," I respond. I'm not sure why, but I feel compelled to follow him, as if the universe has orchestrated this moment, as if I couldn't deny my curiosity even if I wanted to.

The walk is short and quiet, but the farther we go on the beach, the darker it becomes, and that's when I notice it: a large light in the distance, an iridescence sitting before a small fire. As we walk closer, it dims, and another one next to it starts to glow.

I can't tell if I'm going crazy, maybe it's just the flames from the firepit in the wind, maybe a strange reflection.

Either way, I'm here.

Be calm... Don't shimmer...

"Welcome, I'm Dustin. By the way, I know it's a lot to take in, but grab a seat," he offers warmly.

I take a seat next to him, and a girl with jet-black hair, who introduces herself to me as Emily.

"Welcome! What's your name? Tell us a bit about yourself." Emily says enthusiastically, gesturing to the fire, causing my eyes to wander to several members of the group.

Did I imagine it?

I thought I saw...

He said there were others...

The panic starts, the warmth rushes in; I clamp down on my journal, but I can't control it.

I shut my eyes tightly, not wanting to embarrass myself by letting my inner light shine.

No, I can't let them see it.

I absolutely cannot glow!

All I can hear is laughter. I feel like I'm shrinking. I feel so small.

A hand touches my shoulder, and a newly familiar voice enters my head, "Open your eyes, Spencer." The voice chuckles out.

My blood is boiling; I know I must be absolutely chrome.

Brushing his hand off my shoulder, I take a deep breath and open my eyes. I'm ready to destroy him for bringing me here to be the butt of their joke, but what I see stops me instantly.

Their chuckles are accompanied by astonishing lights, some flickering, some steady, with no rhyme or rhythm, but they all, including Dustin, glow.

"So, you were saying?" Emily chuckles out.

I can't help but join in on their laughter.

"Hi, my name is Spencer, and I glow."

"Your glow isn't a flare for the world to mock; it's a beacon for your tribe to find you. Stop dimming for those who prefer the dark."

Fragments

I t all started with a teacup.

A discarded porcelain antique lying on the pavement, its glitter chrome rim catching my eye as I'm stopped at a red light.

I felt like it was calling out for me to bring it home, and I couldn't resist.

I needed to have it.

I circled my car back around and checked my surroundings before I hopped out and scooped it up, not wanting anyone to notice, I'm not in favor of feeling out of place.

I swore I could sense its vibration as I held it, sitting in my driver's seat, twirling the cup around, looking at its intricate design.

I had never seen anything so beautiful; I knew it was meant to be mine.

As I drove home, it's all I could think about, sneaking gazes at it while also trying to focus on the road.

Why would anyone ever toss out something so alluring?

Who could dispose of something so blatantly rare?

As soon as I returned home, I rushed inside my apartment and cleaned it, splashing my new piece in suds and bubbles until its dirt and grime were washed away.

A sense of pride rushed over me as I held my shiny new teacup out in front of me, and I swear its essence got stronger.

I spoke to it like a friend, because to me, in that moment, it was.

"I think you're quite beautiful, chips and all, you know it's our differences that make us unique, right teacup? Right!" I say smiling, looking to find its new space.

Placing the cup in my glass cupboard, I stare at it for a moment before walking away, and that's when the feelings came rushing back in. I'm suddenly drowning in the emotions I had before I found the shiny antique drinkware on the pavement not too long ago.

Walking through my apartment on autopilot, I somehow find myself in front of my dirty bathroom mirror, sighing and staring lifelessly, suffocated by my thoughts.

I wish someone would see the beauty in me.

I would kill to be the teacup.

They see the cracks and that I'm broken, but the beauty, that they never see.

I swore that day my items would never feel that way; they would always feel cherished; they will always feel loved.

That's where the hunt began. I would drive, collect, clean and polish, sharing the vibrations the items brought to me, feeling them love me back.

There were cups, dolls, trinkets, and figurines, and they were all special; they all had their own soul breathing deep within.

The items became my life; I would only leave to hunt, to collect, to fill my empty space.

But the inevitable happened: the items were starting to become a hoard, an obstacle, no longer a beautiful display.

I knew I needed to take action; the thoughts came messily swirling in as usual, and that's when it happened. The teacup, my first piece, fell and shattered to pieces on my wooden floor.

Heart racing at the sight, I rushed over to it, picking up the fragments, not caring if I got nicked by the shards.

As I scooped up the remnants, an idea floated to me, as if the universe meant this all along. I put the porcelain pile to the side and grabbed the glue gun from my cupboard and began on my vision, the project that would change my life forever.

I smashed piece after piece of each item, day after day, building and constructing, barely leaving my home.

Every piece I smashed, I felt its energy quivering. I witnessed the items change, but I knew the bigger sculpture would be beautiful, so I stayed focused on my minds design.

All the additions I pieced together helped me focus on the art, on the elegance I was building before me.

The old emotions were getting buried the more that I created, and I no longer felt damaged from the experiences of my past.

If I placed another piece, I could no longer hear them laugh.

If I placed another piece, I no longer felt attacked.

Some might think it isn't healing, but I'm tired of what they think.

The days began to blend, and the sculpture started to grow and expand.

Little broken pieces of porcelain shaping into legs and then a torso, then arms and a head.

The day I thought I finished, I couldn't help but shatter myself. Internally aching, I burst into tears at the sculpture before me; so beautiful, so grand.

But there was something missing: the energetic echo I once felt; the elation the pieces once brought me was no longer there.

Something had to be missing; I had an inner knowing, a way that I could just tell.

I dreaded leaving my home, but I knew I had to do this. My art deserved it; it needed its vibration; it needed its light.

I set out to find a way to bring back the power to my piece. Driving the streets of my small town aimlessly, and confirmation came from the universe.

It came in the form of broken items, catching my eye, and once held, having that beautiful vibration, the one my sculpture currently lacked.

Once the items were collected, I knew what it was missing, and I headed to my apartment and started working on the task, the last addition.

I cracked and smashed pieces, day by day, building, creating until they were finally done.

A gorgeous set of wings, their span breathtaking, their design perfect.

Looking at what I had created, I could feel the energy emanating from them, and I swore I saw an aura, subtle but impacting.

The wings they were stunning, and when I placed the first one, I knew the energy of the piece was close to being restored.

Placing the last one on and stepping back, I couldn't help but smile. The piece was powerful, filled with beauty, filled with love.

A human form, genderless and breathtaking, pure energy, an angel.

I sat for a moment and stared at it, and before I knew it, the wings flapped, sending a powerful burst of air through my small apartment.

I couldn't believe what I was seeing as the head turned and my piece came to life. I couldn't move, I couldn't speak, so I just sat and watched, awestruck, utterly stunned.

My body trembled as it spoke, its voice deep and spiritually authoritative, like something from beyond.

"McKenzie, why do you waste your talent here hiding in this place?" It asks, hand gesturing out, emitting a shine.

I swallow hard and try to find an answer, my thoughts like a puddle in my brain.

"The p-people, they aren't nice. They make fun of me." I whimper out.

The sculpture stalls before it speaks.

"Look at me, you created me, every piece repurposed then handled with care, do you not think I am beautiful?" the sculpture asked.

"O-of course I do." I answer.

"Others threw the pieces of me away; they no longer found the items useful once the imperfections took place. You, McKenzie, you are different. You saw beauty in every little thing."

The emotion in me is building, but I sit and continue to listen.

"You see, when things break, you have a choice: you can sit and dwell over the loss of what used to be or pick up the pieces and create something new. That is the beauty of being a creator, the most powerful beauty of all."

I feel a tear roll down my cheek as I watch the sculpture flap its wings.

A warm vibration filled with subtle color brushes over me, and the figure returns to its original stance, frozen in place.

It's hard to put into words what that experience brought me, but I know it gave me courage.

The courage to make my way back to that bathroom mirror and finally wipe it clean.

I stand for a moment just to look at my obviously exhausted expression.

Running my hands through my unkempt onyx hair, I lean in closer and center my focus.

I take a deep breath, and I whisper to my reflection.

"It's time to create something new."

"You can spend your life hiding from the world that threw you away, or you can take every broken piece of your past and build yourself a pair of wings."

Visions

It's hard to pinpoint exactly when it started: my desire to know what awaited me in my future.

It seems like I've always wondered who I would marry, or if I would land the job of my dreams, but more importantly, what path would I take to get there, to ultimately make my dreams come true.

It seemed like a miracle when I met Miss Clara. I would go in for weekly readings, then daily until she finally got sick of me, I'm assuming, and gave me a tool of my own.

I was hesitant at first. I didn't have a gift, or a spark, or whatever these oracles have that grants them the ability to see into the unknown.

She assured me that everyone was magical, and to access my inner magic, I just had to believe; I had to really internally desire to see what was ahead of me, and it would be revealed.

She told me I had power.

The crystal ball sat on my nightstand for weeks before I touched it, afraid of what it might say, but without my usual readings from Miss Clara, I was going crazy not knowing what might happen next.

Anything could occur; danger could be waiting around the corner, or maybe today would be the day I got a pleasant surprise.

I had to stop wondering; I had to know.

It took a lot of courage to pick up the reflective sphere in my hands; its weight alone made it feel powerful, and the light bouncing from it was entirely majestic. It's pretty hard to explain, but I just knew it belonged to me.

The first time I sat with it and held it tight, I closed my eyes and thought of my question. I asked it if I would ever find the love of my life. I meditated with that question for what felt like forever, but when I opened my eyes, I saw nothing. The ball was lifeless; no images to be interpreted, no peek into the future.

I grew frustrated, but I trusted Miss Clara. She had already told me my dreams would come true after several of our visits, but it's been so long, and I'm stuck in the same place. I know if she says this ball will work, it will. I can feel its power. I just have to try harder. I close my eyes and ask a more open-ended question.

I ask it: What will happen tomorrow?

When I open my eyes, the light emanating from the ball is almost blinding before it slowly dims. The energy within is gently vibrating through my hands as I watch the tiny images come to life.

I see myself in my glittery red dress, at a dinner, sitting at a table, waiting alone. In walks my sister, who joins me and takes a seat, looking troubled, her face pale, her eyes red and glossy as though she'd been crying for days.

I haven't seen my sister in years...

This can't be right...

Just as the thoughts start to float in and my mind is whirling with wonder, the ball fully dims, followed by the alert on my phone.

I go to check the notification, and of course, it's my sister, telling me she wants to talk, and she asks if I would be open to meeting with her. I sent a simple text to agree.

Meeting with her the next day felt like a dream, like I was stuck in a daze. I listened to her talk about her divorce, but I felt absent and could predict what she would say next. I didn't mention the crystal ball to her; she never liked anything to do with magic, and I was only there to support her, anyway.

I continued to consult the ball day by day.

Every day felt surreal, like I was out here existing, but I wasn't really living. I was in an endless loop of chasing predictions until something broke the flow.

I started getting visions without consulting the ball.

These visions were different; they didn't come with the numbness that already knowing provides. The glimpses into the future made me feel alive, more than I've been in a very long time.

It would happen at the strangest moments, when I would go about my day doing mundane tasks on autopilot, just floating through the familiar. A neon flash would abruptly pop into my vision, giving me a clip of myself in various situations, always happy and super content.

I felt as though the visions were taunting me, showing me the life I really wanted.

In this other life, I had the perfect spouse, a beautiful home, and a great bond with my kids. I needed this to be my reality, not a glitch that popped in and out, showing me things that don't currently exist.

The crystal ball was my only hope. I would ask it a question, trying to get any additional information on my visions, but it would never react. I continued to preview my days, hoping maybe one day the real vision I want could be in the ball on display.

The quest felt hopeless as the neon glimpses kept coming, but my reality remained unchanged.

I needed to find an answer; the weight was becoming too much to bear. I decided to go back to where it all started, to Miss Clara, to gain answers on how to merge my futures to create the life I saw.

I felt as though the universe had completely turned its back on me when I finally arrived at her shop. A closed sign hung in the window, and all of her items were gone from their displays.

When I returned home, I felt hopeless.

Why can't I have the future I want?

Where I'm happy and living; truly living?

The more I thought about the neon glimpses, the more enraged I became.

Looking over at my nightstand, I saw the ball sitting in all its glory, its presence provoking and sinister, gleaming, not a worry to its name.

It's all your fault...

It was bound to happen; I couldn't let it stay. This crystal ball, this oracle's tool, destroyed my life, and it was time to pay.

I stomp over to it with intention, to shatter it and find healing when it breaks.

The theme of my life must be wrapped around things not going as planned, because as I approach the ball in anger, I'm compelled by its presence; I'm frozen in place.

I can't do it...

I still need it...

Not everything is predictable, a lesson I should've well learned by this point. But it doesn't help ease the feeling of myself breaking, when the ball moves on its own and shatters on the ground, setting itself free, all of its visions erased.

I try to pull myself together, but the neon flash returns; it's him once again, my partner in the future, smiling and happy, holding our child's hand.

It's the last vision I got for a while, and the days went by as they used to, before the magic, before the ball.

I admit that I miss them, my tiny peeks into the future, but I do feel somewhat free.

It's funny that when things start to feel back in order, you know it's about to get a little strange.

It was a normal morning, and I woke up with a feeling in my stomach, warm and tingling, and I had it all day. I went about my routine as usual, but when I was taking out the trash at work, my life forever changed.

The man from my premonitions was walking up to me, his clothes exactly as I had seen him in a vision once before.

His voice was kind and welcoming. We chatted a bit, shared a few chuckles, and exchanged numbers before I had to head back in.

"I like your necklace." He complimented, as I was walking in on my way back to my boring job.

I look down and twirl the tiny crystal ball in my hands as I smile and thank him in reply.

His last words sent a shiver through my body so intense I knew it came from somewhere different, from the universe itself.

"You know, you don't need a crystal ball; sometimes the things you're looking for find you when you just stop searching." He yelled out with a chuckle.

I walk back into work and sit at my station, no longer missing not knowing, happy with it all.

I remove my necklace and toss it into the trash next to my station.

That was my last consultation with any crystal ball.

"There is a certain kind of magic in the unknown, a quiet peace in realizing that some things are better felt than foreseen."

The Special Ingredient

Some things you just get used to; they become so familiar that you feel as if you are on autopilot, just living the same day over and over, waiting for something big to happen, waiting for a change.

Working at The Salted Grill was no different; I would create the same recipes and use the same high-end ingredients, just to please the critics and the elite clientele. They were in love with the aesthetic, the ornate ambiance, which gave them that feeling of being supposedly better than the people who couldn't afford to eat here; the thought made me sick.

Many would think I stayed here for the pay, but that wasn't it; I wanted to earn that Michelin star, to finally feel like I have accomplished something great. So, I fell into the system, creating dish after dish with precision, ensuring the result was always the same. The years went by, and I'm still here, no star, just self-loathing for choosing to remain in a place that revels in the idea of being elite; the very thing I despise.

Sundays were my favorite days. It was when I was finally free to create meals in the way I truly desired. I was no longer bound by strict recipes that lacked emotion in their taste.

Despite the exhaustion from a prior week of panning out dishes for the uppity customers at The Salted Grill, I would find time to volunteer at a local soup kitchen, where my culinary prowess could truly shine. I had a unique love for the missionary kitchen, one that I could never find at the job where I spent most of my time. The staff was friendly and loved to craft new things, and I loved seeing the residents smile when they dined.

My gift was free here, a talent I've held secret for years. Food was more than just sustenance to me; each item carried an energy, one that I could always sense deeply. The way the vibration of a potato had the potential to heal a broken heart when paired with an elegant wine. How a single dash of turmeric could stop tears from falling when added to a stew. I never knew how I gained this ability, but I somehow kept it through the years, crafting specific recipes with my eager energy to bring love and warmth to souls in need.

I stirred my pot with purpose, the need to heal the hurt I could feel emanating from people in the soup kitchen, most of whose hearts were calling for comfort and relief. I thought about how I wanted them to feel better, about how everyone deserves happiness, and wished it toward them, even if only for a moment. The more I stirred, the more drained I felt, but I knew it was the work I needed to do, stirring for purpose, not to satisfy greedy needs. Sometimes the things that are hard to do are the most meaningful, a lesson I learned quickly as I aged over the years.

Today felt very different as I set up the stations and the lines began to form. I noticed an older woman at a back table, hunched over and alone. There was something distinct about her, it's like I not only sensed her energy but I slightly saw her aura. It was beyond beautiful.

I made her a plate of tonight's meal, roast beef over mashed potatoes, vibrating with the energy of love. She looked nervous as I walked over to her, her eyes darting from me to the ground. I offered her a greeting, hoping to lighten the energy a bit, to make her feel more comfortable.

"Hello, I'm Aiden," I introduced myself, hoping she'd open up and maybe share her name.

She sat silently, so I offered her the plate and sat with her, curious to see her reaction to my meal.

At first, she was reluctant to eat, but eventually she picked up her fork and began to take bites. I watched as her expression changed from sullen to joyous; she was now wearing a slight grin. She looked up from her plate and smiled at me from ear to ear before she spoke.

"This reminds me of my Aunt Carol's roast. I haven't thought of her for years. This is delicious." She exclaimed, her voice sweet and warm.

I thank her and rise from the table, but she grabs my hand softly and gives me a few parting words.

"You know, you are extremely talented. You should consider working at a restaurant; this is Michelin-star quality." She compliments before letting go of my arm and continuing to eat.

I thank her and make my way back to the serving station to help the rest of the staff.

The next day at work was daunting; it was the usual routine. I sent out dish after dish of the same boring recipes, the ingredients for which I've lost taste for so long ago. I was plating a roasted chicken breast when I saw my boss stomp over to me furiously, so I took a deep breath before we were finally face-to-face.

"They sent this back, Aiden, too much salt! We have a strict recipe to adhere to; they are repeat customers, so I know you did something you weren't supposed to, and that's not how we function here at The Salted Grill! We pride ourselves on precision."

I watch silently as he makes an ostentatious display, emptying the full plate of food in the trash and then tossing the dish in the sink.

A moment of awkward silence lingered between us. The universe had other plans for me that day. I felt a heat rise in my chest, and for some reason, I thought of the lady from yesterday, how her face glowed, how she was genuinely thankful for the dish I made. As he's walking away, I shout out a reply.

"Then maybe the Salted Grill isn't the place for me!" I bark out, taking off my apron and throwing it into the trash.

"You can't just walk out mid-shift! If you do this, you'll never work in another restaurant in town! We are top-notch around here! You'd better think about your—" his words fade as I ignore him and continue my way out the kitchen doors and head home.

I spent the next few days in the soup kitchen, offering help to make the days go by a little quicker and bring smiles to the residents' faces. Fortunately enough, working for so long at The Salted Grill had given me enough savings to survive for a while until I came up with a plan. The days went by, and I looked for the lady, the one who loved my pot roast, but she never showed. I continued to volunteer, feeding the community, sharing my gift, and spreading love.

It's funny how destiny just comes knocking when we least expect it. It banged my door hard when I was walking home from the soup kitchen one day, and I saw a space for rent in an alley not too far from my apartment. I felt like it was mine, like it was written in the stars, and it turns out that it was. I applied, got approved, and began setting up a quaint little sit-in of my own.

"Aiden's Ladle", the sign read, and it felt like home. The customers came and went, some familiar, surprisingly, from The Salted Grill, probably chasing an experience they heard about by word of mouth. The days went by, and it must've been a few weeks, and I finally saw her, the lady from the soup kitchen, the one who loved my roast.

Elated to see her, I went over and personally brought her a dish, hoping to strike up a conversation, just glad to see her again. As I sat down with her, this time she was the one to start the conversation, her voice decorated with joy. "I see you've found your true calling, Mr. Aiden, no longer cooking for the ones who don't deserve the beautiful gift you have."

"How did you—" I begin to ask, but she instantly cuts me off.

"Some things don't need an explanation; some things are just meant to be." She states matter-of-factly before taking a bite from her fork.

I let her words sit with me for a moment, but then I had to know.

"May I ask your name?" I question.

"Me, darling? My name is Fate, and you met me long ago."

"The most important lesson I learned wasn't in a recipe book: you can't feed the world until you've finally fed yourself."

Recipes

✧ ✧ ✧

□ *Recipes for a Magical Life* □

✧ ✧ ✧

Hey there, Stardust,

Welcome.

In the upcoming section, you will find gentle tools to help you through the days that feel a little too overwhelming.

These tips are dressed up as recipes, created to nourish your soul in the same way food nourishes the body. Just as we need fuel to keep moving, the health of the mind and mindful awareness are just as essential.

Feed both your body and your soul so that each day you can continue to radiate your own magical glow.

Bon Appétit,

- **J.J. Ems**

Recipe for Happiness

"Happiness is only a memory away."

Some days can be rough. Whenever you feel like things are hopeless, try to remember the good times.

There will be better days.

✧ ✧ ✧

☾ Recipe for Happiness ☽

✧ ✧ ✧

<u>Prep Time:</u> A few quiet moments to sift through pleasant memories

<u>Yield:</u> Unlimited; use until satiated

<u>Ingredients:</u>

• A favorite childhood memory

• A warm blanket or a comfortable seat

• Calm breathing

• A comforting fragrance of choice (tip: food scents are often linked with positive experiences, such as bakery or coffee shop aromas)

• Gratitude for taking time for yourself

<u>Instructions:</u>

Get comfortable, whether sitting or lying down, and snuggle into your blanket, relishing the feeling of safety.

Slow your breathing with controlled breaths.

Close your eyes and think of a memory from childhood or adulthood that brings you joy. Focus on just one and hold it in your mind.

Let the feeling of happiness wash over you. Imagine it as a soft light starting at your toes and gently brushing upward, filling your body with warmth while pushing away worry.

Continue this process as long as you need. Relive the memory and walk away knowing there are many more positive moments to create.

You are magical after all!

<u>Best Enjoyed With:</u>

Music or foods associated with the memory, if any.

<u>Side effects may include:</u>

- ◆ A sense of relief
- ◆ An urge to create new memories
- ◆ Gratitude for your past

Recipe for Forgiveness

"The moment you choose to forgive is also the moment you choose to heal."

Not every day will be perfect. Some days will test you. You may get angry, and you might make decisions you regret.

When those moments happen, remember to forgive others, but most importantly, forgive yourself.

✧ ✧ ✧

☾ Recipe for Forgiveness ☽

✧ ✧ ✧

Prep Time: A few moments to breathe and let go.

Yield: Unlimited; use until healed

Ingredients:

• A setting where you feel free. This one doesn't require quiet. Turn on music or have a show playing if you like.

• A notebook

• A writing utensil

• A treat of any kind (optional)

Instructions:

Sit and get comfortable.

Use a controlled breathing method of your choice.

Write out your feelings surrounding the situation. Let it be messy. Draw, scribble, or write whatever comes naturally. The goal is to release the emotion onto the page.

When you feel finished, crumple the paper. Let the emotion go and throw it away.

Take a moment to breathe. Forgive yourself for what happened. If another person is involved, you may choose to forgive them too. It does not have to be forced. If you need more time, you can return to this later.

Now shift the energy. Turn up the music, read a book, or watch a show.

This is where the snack comes in.

Bon appétit, my rebel.

<u>Best enjoyed with:</u> An incense or soothing scent of your choice

<u>Side effects may include:</u>
- ✦ A weight lifted
- ✦ Newfound joy
- ✦ A feeling of self-love.

Recipe for Belonging

"It's common to want to fit in. It's magical when you realize you can create a world of your own."

Life can feel annoying when you feel different. Sometimes it seems like the world was built for people who want to go with the flow.

But you? You're magical.

Take a moment and remember this: you're already here, and you already belong.

✧ ✧ ✧

☾ Recipe for Belonging ☽

✧ ✧ ✧

<u>Prep Time:</u> A little time to remind yourself you're awesome.

<u>Yield:</u> Unlimited; use whenever you need a reminder that you are bad-ass.

<u>Ingredients:</u>

• A setting of your choice (this recipe is all about your inner magic)

• A memory of a fun time with a friend

• Some upbeat music

• A secret ingredient of your choice

<u>Instructions:</u>

This one is unconventional, my friend. This isn't a regular book.

Get into your chosen space.

Bring up that memory with your friend. Let yourself remember how it felt.

Turn the music up. Headphones are a great idea if you want to fully immerse yourself.

Got your secret ingredient?

Now get a little wild. Dance if you want. Move your body. Relive that freedom.

When you're done, notice something important:

That friend you remembered. That moment you shared. None of it was accidental.

That playful energy you just felt is proof that you already know how to connect. That is your magic.

Go out into the world, or go online if that feels safer. You already have the energy needed to attract your people.

<u>Best enjoyed with:</u> an open mind.

<u>Side effects may include:</u>
- ✦ A need to party
- ✦ A feeling of playfulness
- ✦ A magical hangover

Recipe for Inner Peace

"Tranquility can be found in a quiet mind; don't be afraid to shut out the noise and reclaim your peace."

The world is loud. It thrives on your attention. You are not required to give all of yourself.

Step away. Log off. Close the door.

You can't save the world while abandoning yourself.

✧ ✧ ✧

☾ Recipe for Inner Peace ☽

✧ ✧ ✧

<u>Prep Time:</u> A moment where you choose yourself.

<u>Yield:</u> Unlimited; use until the noise loses power.

<u>Ingredients:</u>

• A favorite form of media (movie, show, music, etc.)

• A favorite snack and/or drink

• Incense or a scented candle

• Time carved out for you, no guilt allowed

<u>Instructions:</u>

This is your rebellion, your reclamation of inner peace.

Light the candle or incense as if you're drawing a boundary. Press play like you're shutting the world out.

Whether you sit in silence, dance wildly, or laugh too loud, do it unapologetically.

No expectations. No proving yourself.

This is your time. You deserve every second of it.

Best enjoyed with: friends and/or family.

Side effects may include:
◆ A spark of defiance
◆ A breath that feels deeper
◆ A peaceful state of mind

Recipe for Self-Worth

"The true beauty of being you is that it's something only you can do."

It's easy to measure your worth by trophies, titles, and applause. But you are not basic — you are brilliantly unique. Awards or not.

✧ ✧ ✧

□ ***Recipe for Self-Worth*** □

✧ ✧ ✧

Okay, come on now, my rebellious magician.

Did you really think I was going to hand you a step-by-step guide to recognizing your own worth?

If you've made it this far, you should know me better than that.

You don't need a recipe. You don't need proof. You don't need permission.

You are already enough.

Now go on. Keep rebelling, rock star.

Love and Light,

- **J.J. Ems**

Love Letters

《 *Dear Outcasts* 》

My awesome soul,

Thank you for being brave enough to be bold, different, and daring to embrace change.

I know it's not the easiest path to take. People stare, give us a hard time, and toning it down to fit in can seem tempting.

But we are brave enough to keep fighting, which is why I curated this section just for you.

Within the next pages, you will find letters I've personally written for you when times feel rough, to remind you that you are not alone.

We are in this together, and I hope you find a message here to spark that light and summon that inner fighter we all have inside.

✧You are magical, after all.

With love and light,

And maybe a little chaos.

- **J.J. Ems**

Embrace Uniqueness

Dear unique earth traveler,

I know the world feels difficult when you feel different.

Every corner you turn, and every task you have to complete, can feel as though it was designed to favor those who embrace conformity.

But little do you know, crushing the cookie-cutter is a gift.

The truth is, being different means that in your heart, you are a creator.

You can rise above the standards by crafting your own version of the world, and that is powerful.

If you feel like there isn't a place for you, why not make one?

If you feel like you are alone, you can build your chosen family.

That's the beautiful thing about thinking outside the box. We are all energetically connected and can choose to come together to create change.

I may not know you personally, but I've shared my world with you through these pages, because I, too, feel different.

I also find it hard to be what others perceive as normal, and I feel more comfortable in the outlandish and strange.

I wrote this to let you know, my friend, that you are loved.

Being different can be a chaotic blessing when you choose it to be.

With love and light,

- **J.J. Ems**

Think Freely

Hello, my black sheep,

I want to begin by telling you this: you are beautiful. Too beautiful to fit in.

Sure, we could do what everyone else does. We could aim to please, float through life without asking questions, or quiet the parts of ourselves that feel different.

But we don't.

We are meant for something more, even when that path feels lonely. And although you may feel alone right now, you are not. I am a black sheep, too, and there are many others like us.

While the softer, more desired sheep move easily from flock to flock, we have something different.

We get to build lives that are uniquely our own.

We do not need the fluff.

We do not need to blend in to belong.

I encourage you to seek out those who think outside the box. Those who challenge norms. Those who believe in equality, love, and peace. That world can exist if you are brave enough to create it, or brave enough to search for it.

To your beautiful soul, radiating as oddly as mine, I hope you find your chosen family. There is love waiting for you.

Until then, I hope you find comfort in these pages.

I built them for people like us.

The different. The weird. The strange.

Our wool is beautiful.

And if we stand together, it can never be completely shaved away.

With love and light,

- **J.J. Ems**

You Are a Creator

Hello new friend,

I hope you've been enjoying these pages, and I hope they make you feel right at home. Life is a wild adventure. We learn lessons; we meet people; we grow, and sometimes we move on. But some experiences stay with us, and I wanted to share a piece of advice I once received from a friend.

If you're here, I imagine you're probably like me — one of the outcasts, the black sheep, the rebels.

Being different can be empowering if you choose it to be. But it rarely starts that way. It often begins with feeling anxious, strange, or like you simply don't belong.

I'm all too familiar with those feelings. If I'm being honest, I still feel them sometimes. But I'll never forget what a friend said to me when I was younger. I was sad, searching for meaning in a world that felt empty.

She told me, "Maybe you're just not for people to understand."

That sentence forever changed the way I saw myself. It offered a perspective I had never considered. I still carry it with me to this day.

So let me tell you something clearly:

You don't owe anyone an explanation for who you are.

Be a little strange if you want.

Dye your hair that wild color.

You are a creator.

The more authentic you are, the more the right people will gravitate toward you.

Build the world you want; love yourself for daring to be different.

And, of course,

Stay Magical,

- **J.J. Ems**

You Deserve Everything

See you soon...

Alright, my rebellious glow spirits,

It looks like we've come to the end of Y.A.M Volume One: Shining Your Inner Light. Thank you wholeheartedly for your support, and I truly wish you the best on your journey toward a more magical version of yourself.

Keep your eyes peeled for the next volume in this collection, where we'll go a step further and explore magickal practices such as meditation, manifestation, and rituals.

I hope to see you there.

In the meantime, feel free to scan the QR code on the last page of this book, where you can find more of my creations, including my magickal newsletter, articles, and stories.

And remember... don't you dare dim your light.

Until next time,

Love and light,

- **J.J. Ems**

Scan Here for Magic

www.ingramcontent.com/pod-product-compliance
Lightning Source LLC
Chambersburg PA
CBHW051132160726
47997CB00019B/2347